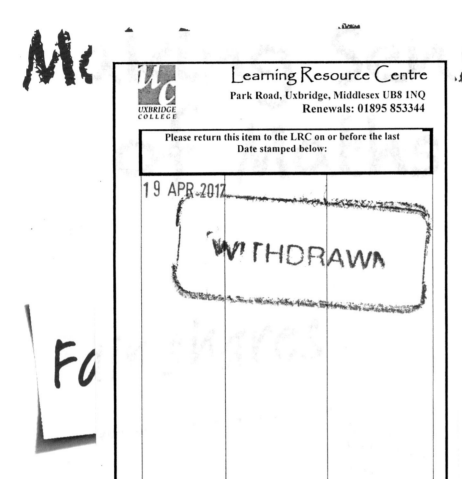

HODDER
EDUCATION

The publishers would like to thank the following for permission to reproduce copyright material:

Photo credits: page 2 © Paul Dickinson; Page 3 t © Māris Kūlis – Fotolia; page 3 b © Stockbyte / Getty Images Ltd; page 4 © tomalu – Fotolia; page 5 t © Stockbyte / Getty Images Ltd; page 5 b © Māris Kūlis – Fotolia; page 8 all photos © Sue Hough; page 9 © Caitlin Seymour; page 12 © Caitlin Seymour; page 13 t © Design Pics Inc. / Alamy; page 21 t l © Marie-Thérèse GUIHAL – Fotolia; page 21 t r © adisa – Fotolia; page 21 b l © Marie-Thérèse GUIHAL – Fotolia; page 21 b r © Marie-Thérèse GUIHAL – Fotolia; pages 25–33 all photos © Sue Hough; page 34 © Kate Crossland-Page; pages 41–43 all photos © Sue Hough; page 45 t © Sue Hough; page 45 b © Kate Crossland-Page; page 53 t r © Caitlin Seymour; page 53 t l © Stockbyte / Getty Images Ltd; page 53 b l © Caitlin Seymour; page 53 b r © Stockbyte / Getty Images Ltd

t = top, c = centre, b = bottom, l = left, r = right

All designated trademarks and brands are protected by their respective trademarks.

Every effort has been made to trace all copyright holders, but if any have been inadvertently overlooked, the Publishers will be pleased to make the necessary arrangements at the first opportunity.

Although every effort has been made to ensure that website addresses are correct at time of going to press, Hodder Education cannot be held responsible for the content of any website mentioned in this book. It is sometimes possible to find a relocated web page by typing in the address of the home page for a website in the URL window of your browser.

Hachette UK's policy is to use papers that are natural, renewable and recyclable products and made from wood grown in sustainable forests. The logging and manufacturing processes are expected to conform to the environmental regulations of the country of origin.

Orders: please contact Bookpoint Ltd, 130 Milton Park, Abingdon, Oxon OX14 4SB. Telephone: (44) 01235 827720. Fax: (44) 01235 400454. Lines are open 9.00–5.00, Monday to Saturday, with a 24-hour message answering service. Visit our website at www.hoddereducation.co.uk

© Paul Dickinson, Stella Dudzic, Frank Eade, Steve Gough, Sue Hough 2012

First published in 2012 by
Hodder Education, an Hachette UK company,
338 Euston Road
London NW1 3BH

Impression number 5 4 3 2
Year 2016 2015 2014

Cover photo © elnariz – Fotolia
Illustrations by Pantek Media, Maidstone, Kent
Typeset in ITC Stone Informal by Pantek Media, Maidstone, Kent
Printed in Spain

A catalogue record for this title is available from the British Library

ISBN 978 1444 169089

Contents

Chapter 4: Multiplication and division

Introduction

These books are intended to help you to make sense of the maths you do in school and the maths you need to use outside school. They have already been tried out in classrooms, and are the result of many comments made by the teachers and the students who have used them. Students told us that after working with these materials they were more able to understand the maths they had done, and teachers found that students also did better in tests and examinations.

Most of the time you will be working 'in context' – in other words, in real-life situations that you will either have been in yourself or can imagine being in. For example, in this book you will be looking at sharing pizzas, installing computer packages, and necklace designs, among many other things.

You will regularly be asked to 'draw something' – drawings and sketches are very important in maths and often help us to solve problems and to see connections between different topics. This is certainly the case for the work on fractions, percentages, ratio, decimals and proportion.

You will also be expected to talk about your maths, explaining your ideas to small groups or to the whole class. We all learn by explaining our own ideas and by listening to and trying out the ideas of others.

Finally, of course, you will be expected to practice solving problems and answering examination questions.

We hope that through working in this way you will come to understand the maths you do, enjoy examination success, and be confident when using your maths outside school.

Work experience

1 As part of a work experience project, Aisha, Sandra, Ben and Mike are each put in charge of a small group of primary children on a school trip. The school has provided sandwiches for the primary children. These have to be shared out equally. The teacher in charge asks Aisha and the others to make sure that this is done fairly.

Aisha has four children in her group and has been given three sandwiches to share equally between them.

This is what is happening in the other groups:

Sandra's group   Ben's group   Mike's group

The next day, some parents complain that not all pupils got the same amount to eat. Put the groups in order, starting with the group that had the most to eat.

2 Use drawings to show how Aisha, Ben, Sandra and Mike could share out their sandwiches fairly within their groups.

 Now complete Workbook exercise 1.1 on pages 1–2 of your workbook.

3 Each primary pupil also takes a plastic bottle of water that they are expected to drink during the trip.

I've already drunk about $\frac{1}{4}$ of my water

I've drunk a third of mine.

George   Hallie

 Use this information to complete Workbook exercise 1.2 on pages 3–5 of your workbook.

Pablo's pizzas

4 Pablo ran a family pizza restaurant in Rome for many years. He was famous for making 'Pizza al Taglio', which are huge rectangular pizzas that groups of people share between them.

When he moved to the UK and opened his first restaurant, he was told that people here are used to circular pizzas. He decided to offer both circular and rectangular pizzas on the menu. A section of the menu is shown here.

Menu

Circular Pizza		Rectangular Pizza	
12" (30 cm)	£6	16" (40 cm)	£8
16" (40 cm)	£8	24" (60 cm)	£12
20" (50 cm)	£10	30" (75 cm)	£14

Vikki and three of her friends decide to share a circular 16" (40 cm) Pablo Special between them.

What measurement of the pizza is 16" (40 cm)?

5 Draw a sketch of the pizza and show how Vikki might cut it so that each person gets the same amount.

6 The pizza costs £8. How much should each person pay?

7 A party of 24 people arrive at Pablo's restaurant. They are seated at three tables, with eight people at each table. At the first table, Ben orders five circular 16" (40 cm) Pablo Specials to share between them.

When the five pizzas arrive there is an argument about how best to cut them so that each person gets the same amount.

Draw a sketch of the pizzas and show how they could be cut so that each of the eight people gets the same amount.

8 Someone at another table asks Ben how much pizza he has got. How would you describe how much pizza Ben has on his plate?

9 The second table also orders five circular 16" pizzas between the eight people. After 20 minutes the pizzas still haven't arrived and they are starting to get hungry. The waiter says that two of their pizzas are ready, but they will have to wait for the others.

I can give you two of your pizzas now, then the other three later

Ok, but I'm not sure how we will share them out. Everybody is really hungry!

They decide to share out the two pizzas equally now, and then share out the other three pizzas when they arrive.

Draw a sketch of the pizzas to show how they will do this.

10 How much does each person get out of the first two pizzas?

11 How much does each person get out of the other three pizzas?

12 Did the people at both tables eat the same amount of pizza? Explain your answer.

13 The third table of eight people orders six circular 16" pizzas between them. When they arrive (all together!) they share the six pizzas equally. Peter says, 'I have $\frac{1}{2}$ of a pizza on my plate and also $\frac{1}{4}$ of a pizza.'

Draw a sketch to show how the pizzas are shared out at this table.

14 Peter says, 'We had more at this table than the others did.' Make a drawing to show how much more the people on Peter's table got.

15 A few weeks later, Ben visits the restaurant again, this time with four of his friends. First they have to decide whether to order circular or rectangular pizzas.

    a) Draw a circular pizza and a rectangular pizza and divide each one into five **equal** parts.

    b) Which would you choose: circular or rectangular? Give a reason for your answer.

16 They eventually decide to order a 30" (75 cm) rectangular pizza.
What measurement on the pizza is 30" (75 cm)?

17 Draw a sketch to show where Ben could slice the pizza so that each person gets an equal amount.

18 What fraction of the pizza does each person get?

19 30" pizzas cost £14. How much should each person pay for their share?

Coley the cutter

Table 1

20 Coley works in Pablo's restaurant on Saturdays. His job is to cut the pizzas before they arrive at the tables. But what he enjoys most is listening to the arguments when the bill arrives. One Saturday night was particularly good for this.

The three people at Table 1 ordered a 40 cm rectangular pizza cut into ten equal pieces. The total cost was £8.

a) How many pieces did Amy eat?

b) How many pieces did Joe eat?

c) How much should each person pay towards the final bill?

Table 5

21 The three people on Table 5 ordered a 60 cm rectangular pizza costing £12.

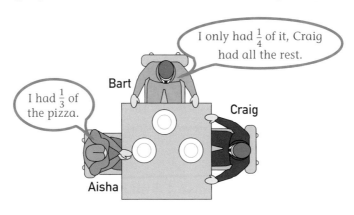

Coley couldn't remember how many pieces he had cut this pizza into. Here are some possibilities.

Cut into 8 pieces:

Cut into 12 pieces:

Cut into 15 pieces:

a) How many pieces do you think Coley had cut this pizza into? Give a reason for your answer.

b) How much of the pizza did Craig have?

c) How much of the pizza did Aisha and Bart have altogether?

d) Aisha paid for herself and for Bart. Craig paid for himself. How much should Aisha and Craig each pay towards the final bill?

Table 7

㉒ At Table 7, Dale ate $\frac{1}{2}$ of a pizza, Ellen ate $\frac{1}{4}$ of it and Frankie ate $\frac{1}{6}$ of it.

a) How many pieces do you think the pizza was sliced into?

b) Was all the pizza eaten? Give a reason for your answer. How much was left over, if any?

 Now do Workbook exercise 1.3 on pages 6–8 of your workbook.

Pizza fractions

23 When Coley gets back to school on Monday, he uses his work at the restaurant to help him with some questions on fractions.

The teacher's question is:

$$\textbf{Work out } \frac{1}{2} + \frac{1}{3}$$

Coley thinks of this as someone having $\frac{1}{2}$ of a pizza and their friend having $\frac{1}{3}$ of it. He needs to work out how much they have had altogether.

He says:

This would be easiest if I'd sliced the pizza into 12 pieces.

So the person eating $\frac{1}{3}$ would get 4 pieces, and the person eating $\frac{1}{2}$ would get 6 pieces. So altogether they have eaten $\frac{10}{12}$ of the pizza

And he draws:

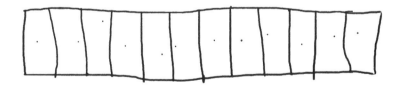

Below his drawings he writes:

$$\frac{1}{2} + \frac{1}{3} = \frac{10}{12}$$

Why did Coley decide to slice the pizza into 12 pieces?

24 Choose a different number of slices and work out the answer to $\frac{1}{2} + \frac{1}{3}$.

25 The next question is $\frac{3}{4} + \frac{1}{6}$. Into how many pieces might Coley imagine slicing the pizza for this question?

26 Make a drawing to show how the pizza was sliced.

27 If one person ate $\frac{3}{4}$ of the pizza and the other person ate $\frac{1}{6}$ of the pizza, how much pizza did they eat altogether?

28 How much more did one person eat than the other?

29 Write down the answers to:

a) $\frac{3}{4} + \frac{1}{6}$

b) $\frac{3}{4} - \frac{1}{6}$

 Now do Workbook exercise 1.4 on pages 9 and 10 of your workbook.

30 So far, Coley has answered all the questions correctly, but he struggles with the next one. The question is:

$$\frac{3}{4} + \frac{2}{5}$$

Make a drawing for this question and try to explain why Coley found it more difficult. What do you think the answer should be?

31 Make up a story from the pizza restaurant for:

$$1\frac{3}{4} + 1\frac{2}{3}$$

32 Work out the answer to:

$$1\frac{3}{4} + 1\frac{2}{3}$$

33 Back at Pablo's restaurant there is a problem. The children's menu allows them to order fractions of a pizza. So, for example, you can order $\frac{1}{2}$ or $\frac{3}{4}$ of a pizza.

Now, Pablo is great at making pizzas but not so good at taking orders.

Table 2 and Table 3 ordered their pizzas at the same time. Pablo thinks all the pizzas are for one table, so he delivers $4\frac{1}{2}$ pizzas to Table 2. However, $1\frac{3}{4}$ pizzas should have gone to Table 3.

a) Draw a picture of the $4\frac{1}{2}$ pizzas and shade the pizzas to be given to Table 3.

b) Use your drawing to work out the actual order for Table 2.

c) Use your drawing to work out $4\frac{1}{2} - 1\frac{3}{4}$.

34 Work out the answers to:

a) $2\frac{2}{3} - 1\frac{1}{3}$

b) $3\frac{1}{2} - 1\frac{1}{4}$

c) $4\frac{3}{4} - 2\frac{2}{3}$

Summary

This chapter has been concerned with fractions and with the idea of 'fair shares'. You have used a bar model to help with comparing fractions and with adding and subtracting. The bar in this section was originally a sub sandwich, a water bottle, or a rectangular pizza. You will meet this model again in other sections of this book.

When adding or subtracting fractions, it is useful to think about Coley slicing pizzas for people in the restaurant.

So, for example, when asked to work out $\frac{1}{4} + \frac{2}{5}$, Coley says:

If one person wants $\frac{1}{4}$ of the pizza and one wants $\frac{2}{5}$, it would be easiest to slice the pizza into 20 pieces. One will get 5 slices and the other will get 8 slices. Altogether they will eat $\frac{13}{20}$ of the pizza.

And he draws:

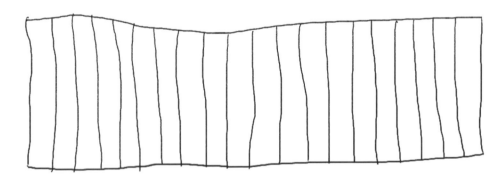

So: $\frac{1}{4} + \frac{2}{5} = \frac{13}{20}$

Downloading programs

1 Demi has won £2000 in a caption competition to explain why she likes to start the day with Rice'o'Pops. She decides to buy a new computer with some of the money. When she gets it home she begins to install some software onto it.

She starts with some anti-virus software. After a few minutes this is what is on her screen:

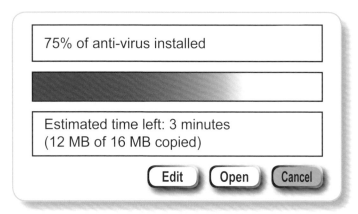

75% of anti-virus installed

Estimated time left: 3 minutes
(12 MB of 16 MB copied)

Edit   Open   Cancel

a) What information is there in this window?

b) How long has Demi got left to wait?

c) How long has she been waiting so far?

d) How many megabytes (MB) are there left to load?

2 Demi has got younger brothers and sisters so she decides to install a Web Filter. The instructions say that the software takes 10 minutes to install and the program is 40 megabytes in size.

a) Draw the window that will be showing after 5 minutes.

b) Draw the window that will be showing after 2.5 minutes.

c) Draw the window that will be showing after 1 minute.

3 Demi now starts to install Microsoft Word. This program only tells you what percentage has already been installed. After 3 minutes she looks at the window. The program has so far only installed 10%.

She decides to phone her friend, Rene, but wonders how long she will have to wait.

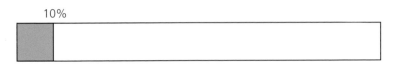

10%

a) How long does this program take to install?

b) How much longer will it be before it is 100% installed?

Over the rest of the day, Demi installs other programs onto her new computer. In Workbook exercise 2.1 on pages 11–12 of your workbook there are nine bars, one for each of the nine programs that she installs. For each program, work out the total installation time.

4 Demi bought her computer from Computers R Us, a new shop that guarantees to be the cheapest. If you can buy the same computer from another shop for less, Computers R Us will give you your money back.

Demi paid £525 for her computer. She decides to check on the internet to see if she can find her computer cheaper somewhere else.

She finds that some shops are having a sale. At PC Universe she sees her computer in the 20% off sale. Its normal price was £660. She decides to work out the sale price to see if it is less than she paid. This is what she does:

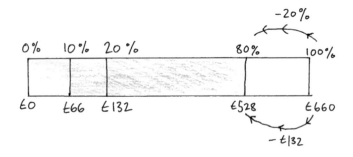

a) Explain in detail Demi's method for calculating the sale price.

b) In what order did she fill in the numbers on the bar?

c) Is the price at PC Universe more or less than at Computers R Us?

5 Next she sees the same computer in PC Solutions. The price is £620, but they have got a 15% off sale.

   a) Draw a bar and use Demi's method to work out the sale price of the computer.

   b) How much more is the price at PC Solutions than at Computers R Us?

6 Demi's friend Rene sees the same computer for sale on the internet. It costs £680 but has 20% off. This is what Rene does to work out the sale price:

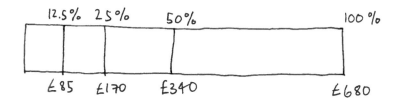

   a) Explain in detail Rene's method for calculating the sale price.

   b) In what order did she fill in the numbers on the bar?

   c) Why would finding 10% help her to work out 20%?

   d) Why does this method not help her to find 10%?

   e) Use Demi's method of finding 10% on the bar to work out the cost of this computer.

 Demi goes on to check out the sale prices for her computer at lots of different shops. Go to Workbook exercise 2.2 on page 13 of your workbook and work out the sale price at each of these shops.

7 At Computers Unlimited, Demi notices that there is 9% off in the sale. Her computer's normal price here was £580. Again, she decides to work out the sale price to see if it is less than she paid. This is what she does:

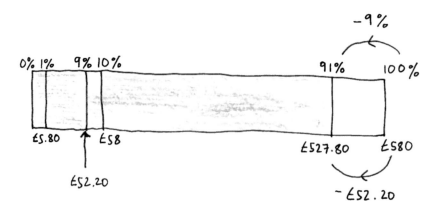

a) Explain in detail Demi's method for calculating the sale price. In what order did she fill in the numbers on the bar? (Demi used a calculator for this one.)

b) Is the price at Computers Unlimited more or less than at Computers R Us?

 Complete Workbook exercise 2.3 on page 14 of your workbook.

8 Look back at **question 7**. Here is a different way of solving the problem:

Percentage	100%	10%	1%	9%
Cost	£580	£58	£5.80	£52.20

$$£580 - £52.20 = £527.80$$

This is called a **ratio table** (you may have used one before).

a) Explain in detail how the ratio table has been used to find a 9% reduction of £580.

b) How is the ratio table similar to the percentage bar used in **question 7**?

c) How is the ratio table different from the percentage bar used in **question 7**?

9 Rene also uses a ratio table to reduce £580 by 9%. This is what she does:

Percentage	100 %	10 %	9 %
Cost	£580	£58	£57

$$£580 - £57 = 523$$

a) Explain what Rene has done differently from Demi.

b) What would you say to Rene to explain why she has gone wrong?

 Complete Workbook exercise 2.4 on page 15 of your workbook.

10 Look at your solutions to **Workbook exercise 2.3** and your solutions to the first five questions of **Workbook exercise 2.4**.

a) What do you notice?

b) Do you prefer to use the percentage bar or the ratio table?

Going to the bank

11 Demi decides to put £1200 of the money that she won into a savings account. At the BarcWest bank they pay 4% interest per year in a normal account and 5% interest per year in a special account. However, in the special account she is not allowed to withdraw any of her money until the end of the year. Demi decides to work out the interest she will get in each account and then decide which account would be best.

a) Work out how much money she will have in the normal account after the interest is paid at the end of the year. You could use a percentage bar like this to help you:

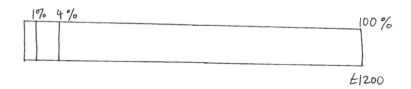

Or you could use a ratio table like this:

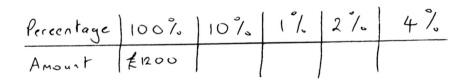

b) Work out how much money she will have in the special account after the interest is paid at the end of the year.

c) How much more interest does she get from the special account?

d) Which of the two accounts would you pick? Explain your answer.

12 Demi goes home and looks at some online bank accounts. Work out how much money she will have in her account after one year of investing £1200 in each of the following banks:

a) E-save account: 6% interest

b) PC Bank: 5.5% interest

c) Big Saver account: 6.5% interest

Test results

13 Demi is convinced that going on revision websites on her new computer is helping her to improve her test marks. Name some websites that she might be using to improve her results.

14 Before she had her computer, Demi got 16 out of 40 in a science test. Her most recent mark in science is 23 out of 50. In which test do you think she got the better mark? Explain your answer.

15 Rene shows Demi how to compare these marks using a percentage bar. To work out 16 out of 40 in Demi's first science test she drew:

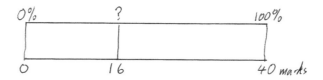

And then:

To work out 23 out of 50 in her recent test she drew:

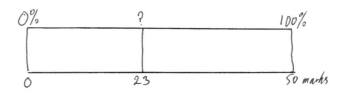

And then:

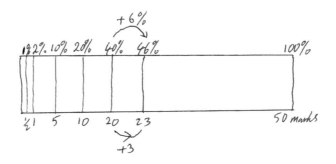

a) Use Rene's bars to explain which test Demi got the better mark in.

b) Demi now sees a quicker way of getting to 46% for science. Can you see a quicker way? What is it?

 Turn to page 16 of your workbook. Use the bars in Workbook exercise 2.5 to work out if Demi has improved in all her lessons.

16 Demi thinks she can also use a ratio table to work out her test percentages. This is what she does for her science mark of 16 out of 40:

Mark	16	8	4	40
Our of	40	20	10	100

So the mark becomes 40 out of 100 or 40%.

Use this method to find her percentage mark in her second science test (23 out of 50).

 Complete Workbook exercise 2.6 on page 17 of your workbook.

Depreciation

17 Sarah is 20 years old and wants to buy her first car. She has saved £2000 to spend and she sees the following four cars for sale for exactly £2000. Each of the cars is 10 years old.

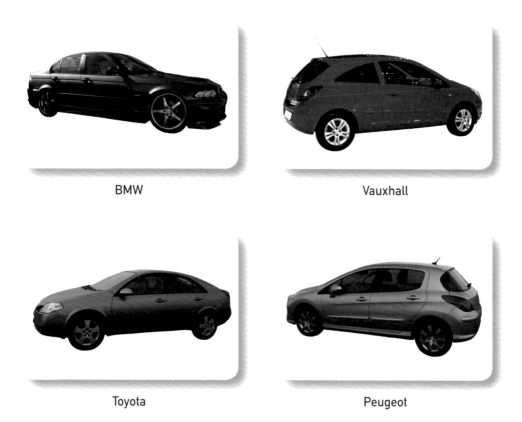

BMW

Vauxhall

Toyota

Peugeot

Which car would you buy? Explain your answer.

18 What advice would you give Sarah to help her pick a car?

19 Sarah has just started a new job and she thinks she will have more money in 3 years' time. She plans to buy a different car in 3 years' time. Her main concern now is how much each car will be worth when she replaces it, so she can use the money to buy a newer car. This is what she finds out about the value of the cars in 3 years' time:

	BMW	Vauxhall	Toyota	Peugeot
Value after 3 years	This car will go down in value by £250 per year.	This car will go down in value by 25% over the 3 years.	This car will be worth half as much in 3 years' time.	After 3 years, this car will be worth 70% of what it was worth at the start.

a) Work out the value of each car in 3 years' time (you may use a ratio table or a percentage bar to help).

b) Which car would be the best one for Sarah to buy?

> When things go down in value they are said to depreciate.

20 Why do you think cars depreciate?

21 Can you think of two other things that depreciate in value?

22 Can you think of two things that do not depreciate in value?

 Complete Workbook exercise 2.7 on page 18 of your workbook.

Summary

When you are answering questions on percentages it is often useful to either draw a **percentage bar** or use a **ratio table**. Here are two examples:

Example 1

Tilly scores 27 out of 60 in a science test. What is her mark as a percentage?

Using a percentage bar:

The test is out of a total of 60. This means 60 marks is 100%.

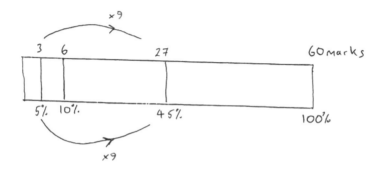

27 marks is 45% so her percentage result is 45%.

Using a ratio table:

Mark	27	9	4.5	45
Out of	60	20	10	100

Tilly's mark is the same as 45 out of 100 so her percentage mark is 45%.

Example 2

The cost of a train ticket from Slough to London Paddington is £8.20. The cost is to be increased by 4%. What will the cost of the new train fare be?

Using a percentage bar:

The cost of the ticket is £8.20 at the moment. This means £8.20 is 100%. We want to find 4% and then add it on.

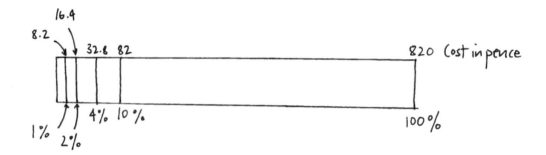

4% is 32.8p. The increase in price will be 33p and the new price will be 820p + 33p = 853p (or £8.53).

Using a ratio table:

Again, the cost of the ticket is £8.20 at the moment. This means £8.20 is 100%. We want to find 4% and then add it on.

Cost in pence	820	82	8.2	16.4	32.8
Percentage	100	10	1	2	4

4% of 820p is 32.8p. The increase in price will be 33p and the new price will be 820p + 33p = 853p (or £8.53).

What's in a necklace?

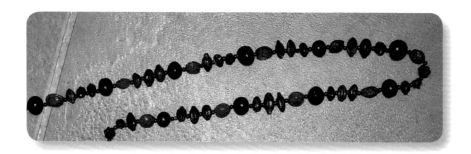

1 **a)** Look at the beaded necklace shown above. Describe in words any patterns you can see in the necklace.

b) Here are the responses of some other students to part **a)**:

Gwen said: 'It's 1 black for every 1 red and 3 brown.'

Sam said: 'It's 3 black to 2 red to 6 brown.'

Scarlett said: 'I think it's 10 black : 10 red : 30 brown.'

i) Find in the picture where you can see each of their ideas.

ii) Decide whether you think their patterns can be correct or not for this necklace.

2 You can't see the entire necklace in this picture, but try to predict the following:

a) If the necklace contains 15 black beads altogether, how many red and how many brown beads do you think it will have?

b) If the necklace contains 54 brown beads altogether, how many black and how many red do you think it will have?

 Turn to your workbook and do Workbook exercise 3.1 on pages 19–20.

The jewellery company

3 Carol and Don decided to set up a small business making beaded necklaces and bracelets. They want to target both the male and female markets with their designs.

As part of their business plan they have conducted some market research. The research looked into what sorts of beaded necklace designs are popular in terms of the colours used and the length of necklace.

One of their first sets of designs is called 'The Monochrome Set'. This is a series of necklaces made up of only black and white beads. The beads are arranged in repeating patterns.

A possible design is shown below:

a) Carol and Don want to target both male and female customers. Suggest some reasons why you think black and white beaded necklaces might be a good seller.

b) Many necklace designers go for repeating patterns in their designs. Suggest some reasons why.

4 Carol and Don start by sketching designs that use a ratio of three white beads to every two black beads.

Here are two partly drawn examples of these designs:

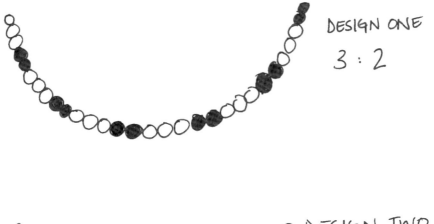

DESIGN ONE

3 : 2

DESIGN TWO

3 : 2

a) Describe in words any patterns you can see in each of the two designs.

b) Show where you can see the 3 : 2 ratio of white to black beads in Design 1.

c) Show where you can see the 3 : 2 ratio of white to black beads in Design 2.

d) Draw a third design based on a white to black ratio of 3 : 2.

e) Carol thinks that there are only two possible different designs for a white to black ratio of 3 : 2. What do you think?

 Turn to pages 21 and 22 in your workbook and do Workbook exercise 3.2.

UXBRIDGE COLLEGE
LEARNING CENTRE

Expanding the business

5 Carol and Don's business does well in its first year.

They decide to extend the range of designs on offer. They also start to make the necklaces in two sizes, short and long.

Here are some samples from their new range of designs.

Design A – Long

Design B – Long

Design C – Long

Design D – Short

Design E – Short

Design F – Short

The price of different types of bead can vary. Carol wants to estimate the cost of beads for each necklace in the designs shown. In order to do this she needs to work out how many of each type of bead is used to make each necklace.

She works on the basis that long necklaces usually contain around 150 beads in total, whereas short necklaces usually contain around 80 beads in total.

Here are her workings out for Design A.

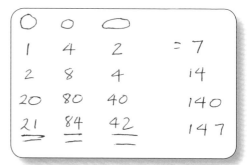

Design A – Long, around 150 beads

a) Describe in words any patterns you can see in the beads.

b) Describe where you can see the numbers she has recorded within the picture.

c) Explain how you think she has come up with her final figures of 21, 84 and 42.

d) Short necklaces are usually made up of around 80 beads in total. Use Carol's method to work out how many of each type of bead would be needed for the short version of Design A.

6 Don is working out how many beads he will need for a short necklace using Design B.

He prefers to use a ratio table.

Here are his workings for Design B:

Rectangle	1	10	2	3
Links	4	40	8	12
Oval	1	10	2	3
TOTAL	6	60	12	18

a) Describe in words any patterns you can see in this necklace.

b) Describe where you can see the numbers 1, 4, 1 and 6 within the picture.

c) How has Don made the other columns in his ratio table?

d) Don wanted to find out how many beads he would need for a short version of Design B. Copy and complete his ratio table.

 Turn to pages 23–24 in your workbook and do Workbook exercise 3.3.

Unthreaded necklaces

7 Two new necklaces from Don and Carol's children's range arrive in their bags unthreaded. These are shown below:

Carol carefully counts the number of each type of bead within each bag.

Bag F contains 30 pink beads and 20 green beads.

Bag G contains 8 blue beads, 12 white beads and 16 lilac beads.

Carol spreads the beads out and tries to work out what each necklace could look like. She knows each one will be based on a repeating pattern.

a) See if you can come up with a possible repeating pattern for the beads in bag F.

b) See if you can come up with a possible repeating pattern for the beads in bag G.

 Turn to pages 25–27 in your workbook and do Workbook exercise 3.4.

Pablo's pizza parlour

8 Kate and Pam have been friends since primary school. They both work in town and regularly meet up for a lunchtime pizza at one of Pablo's restaurants. The lunchtime menu offers large pizzas, ideal for sharing.

One lunchtime they order the ham and pineapple pizza shown above and request that it is cut into eight slices. Kate eats five of the slices, leaving three slices for Pam.

When they get the bill, Kate and Pam like to make sure that each of them pays for what they have eaten.

a) Draw a picture to show how to share out the pizza.

b) Work out how much each person should pay.

9 Kate and Pam decide it is much easier to cut up a rectangular pizza than a round one. So the next week they order the rectangular cheese and tomato pizza shown here. This pizza costs £7.20.

Kate thinks she will want about five pieces, while Pam only wants four. So they decide to cut the pizza into nine equal slices.

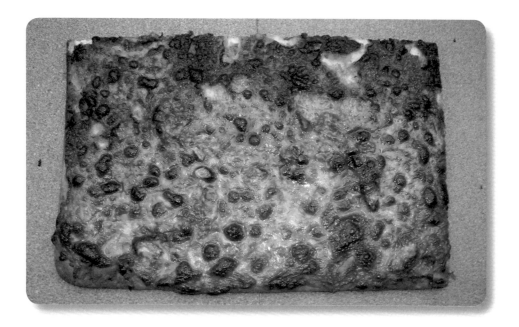

a) Draw a picture to show how to share out the pizza.

b) Share the cost of the pizza between Kate and Pam in the ratio 5 : 4.

10 Here is a copy of the menu for Pablo's pizza parlour.

Pablo's Pizzaria

Made for sharing

Rectangular Pizzas

Cheese & Tomato	£7.20
Ham & Pineapple	£7.60
Pepperoni	£9.50
Vegetarian	£10.20
Seafood	£10.50
Meat Feast	£10.80

a) If you and the person next to you were to share one of these pizzas, decide between you which one you would choose.

b) How would you cut it up?

c) When Kate and her friends go to this restaurant, it is always Kate who works out how to split the bill. Below you can see her calculations on a serviette:

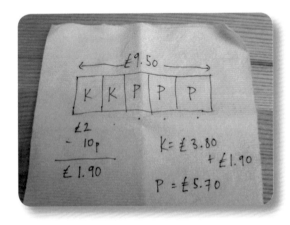

Describe what these calculations tell you about the trip to the restaurant.

d) Which pizza did they have?

 Turn to pages 28–29 in your workbook and do Workbook exercise 3.5.

Using the bar model for ratio problems

11 A teacher was marking test papers for her Year 10 class. One of the questions was:

Share £180 in the ratio 5 : 4

A number of the class had left this question out.

Below you see the strategy used by one of the students:

a) Describe the order in which this student may have written things down.

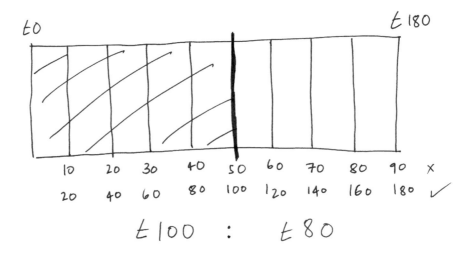

b) Compare this strategy with the method Kate used on her serviette in **question 10**.

c) In both cases a rectangular bar has been drawn. This is known as the 'bar model'. Use a similar method by drawing a rectangular bar to share out a giant, 120 cm length, block of chocolate in the ratio 3 : 5.

 Turn to pages 30–32 in your workbook and do Workbook exercise 3.6.

Who is the fastest of them all?

12 Over the years scientists have measured and recorded the top speeds achieved by various animals.

So the hare is faster than the tortoise?

Or is it?

How do you know?

Look at the list of animals below and try to rank them in order of speed, fastest first.

- Elephant
- Human
- Grizzly bear
- Cheetah

- Greyhound
- Snail
- Lion

- Hare
- Giant tortoise
- Horse

13 **a)** Give some reasons why it is not possible to line these animals up and race them against each other.

b) Make some suggestions as to how you *could* measure the speeds of the various animals.

14 The following table shows some recordings made by scientists.

Elephant	300 metres in 27 s	Lion	400 metres in 18 s
Human	22 metres in 1.8 s	Cheetah	160 metres in 5 s
Horse	500 metres in 25 s	Hare	260 metres in 12 s
Greyhound	400 metres in $22\frac{1}{2}$ s	Grizzly bear	400 metres in 30 s
Snail	12 metres in 15 min	Giant tortoise	136 metres in 30 min

This table can help you decide who was right when you put the animals in order of speed.

a) Were you right with your 1st and 2nd place animals?

b) Were you right with your last and next to last animals?

15 Patricia wanted to find out who was faster between the horse and the greyhound. This is what she did:

Horse

Metres	500	1000
Secs	25	50

Greyhound

Metres	400	800	200	1000
Secs	$22\frac{1}{2}$	45	$11\frac{1}{4}$	$56\frac{1}{4}$

a) Describe what Patricia has done.

b) Explain how this helps Patricia to decide which animal is fastest.

16 Frank does the following work to help him compare the horse and the greyhound.

Horse

Metres	500	100	
Secs	25	5	

Greyhound

Metres	400	200	100
Secs	$22\frac{1}{2}$	$11\frac{1}{4}$	$5\frac{1}{2} + \frac{1}{8} = 5\frac{5}{8}$

a) Describe what Frank has done.

b) Explain how this helps Frank to decide which animal is fastest.

17 Choose some of the animals you were not sure about and use ratio tables to compare their speeds.

18 Find a way to compare the hare and the tortoise. How much faster is the hare than the tortoise?

World record speeds and beyond?

19 The table shows animals recorded over distances in which they achieved their maximum speed. So, for example, the human speed was measured over 22 metres of a 100 m sprint. The lion and the elephant were measured over distances when they were in the act of charging.

Elephant	300 metres in 27 s	Lion	400 metres in 18 s
Human	22 metres in 1.8 s	Cheetah	160 metres in 5 s
Horse	500 metres in 25 s	Hare	260 metres in 12 s
Greyhound	400 metres in $22\frac{1}{2}$ s	Grizzly bear	400 metres in 30 s
Snail	12 metres in 15 min	Giant tortoise	136 metres in 30 min

Frank wonders how the human speed compares with the world record for running 100 metres.

He starts by converting the human speed into metres per second:

Human

metres	22	220	110	12 and a bit
secs	1.8	18	9	1

a) Describe what Frank has done and how he got his figures.

b) Frank is quite surprised by the results for the human. He knows that the world record for sprinting 100 metres is just under 10 seconds. He thinks this is like doing 10 metres in 1 second. The calculation he did above says a human can run around 12 metres in 1 second.

How can you explain this difference?

20 Draw your own ratio tables to help you answer the following questions:

a) Convert the elephant's speed into metres per second. Do the same for the grizzly bear. Who would win that race?

b) How much faster is a horse than a greyhound in metres per second?

c) Compare the lion and the hare's speed in metres per second. What does this tell you?

Animals on the motorway

21 Patricia wonders how the animal speeds compare with the speed of a car. She starts with the fastest animal, the cheetah, and tries to convert this speed into miles per hour.

Cheetah

Metres	160	320	1920	115200	115.2 km
Secs	5	10	60 = 1 min	60 min = 1 hr	1 hr

a) Describe what Patricia has done so far.

b) 5 miles is roughly 8 km. Use this fact to try to convert 115.2 km per hour into miles per hour.

c) Do you think a cheetah's top speed would look out of place on a motorway?

22 a) Choose three other animals from the table and convert their speeds into miles per hour.

b) How much faster is the hare than the tortoise in miles per hour?

c) What about the human speed in miles per hour?

d) Do you think miles per hour is a good way to look at animal speed or not?

Jewellery prices

23 Carol and Don want to expand their business even further. They start looking into selling some of their necklaces in Europe and in America.

They wonder how much to mark up the prices for selling in Europe and in America.

a) Why might they need to charge more for their necklaces in Europe and in America compared with the UK?

b) This necklace retails at £9 in the UK.

Make some suggestions about what price you would put on this necklace:

i) in Europe

ii) in America

(The exchange rates at the time are: £1 = 1.13 Euros; £1 = 1.63 US dollars.)

c) Carol uses a ratio table to help her think about the price. This can be seen below:

£	1	10	9
Euro	1.13	11.3	10.17

£	1	10	9
US dollars	1.63	16.3	14.67

Describe what Carol has done.

d) Carol decides to price the necklace at 12 Euros for the European market and 16 dollars for the American market.

How do these prices compare with your suggestions from part **b)**?

24 The necklace shown below retails at £22 in the UK.

a) Suggest what price to charge in Europe.

b) Suggest what price to charge in America.

25 Carol starts looking in other shops to see what the difference is in prices in the UK compared with other countries.

Here is an example of a ticket price in the UK:

a) How do the prices shown on this ticket compare with the exchange rate of £1 = 1.13 Euros?

b) This item was made by a British company and then sold in other countries in Europe. Based on the exchange rate of £1 = 1.13 Euros, this item has been marked up for the European market. By how much has it been marked up?

c) Why might companies mark up their prices when they sell products abroad?

26 The following price tickets are for a different company:

a) Are the items shown above more expensive to buy in pounds or in Euros?

b) Which ticket is showing the biggest mark-up?

Buying electrical goods in America

27 John is going to America on business. He has heard that some electrical goods are cheaper over there than in the UK. John would like a new iPod. He does some research on the internet, looking at the price of iPods in the UK and in America.

Product	US retail price	UK retail price
iPod Nano	$149	£131
iPod Shuffle	$49	£40
iPod Touch – 8 GB	$229	£193
iPod Touch – 32 GB	$299	£254
iPod Touch – 64 GB	$399	£336

On the day John looks at these prices, the exchange rate is: £1 = $1.59.

a) John looks at these figures and does a quick calculation in his head. He reckons that it will be cheaper to buy these items in America. What do you think he did?

b) Work out how much he could save on each item if he bought it in America.

c) Use the internet to research the prices of some goods that you are interested in. Compare the prices in the UK, America and Europe to find out where they are cheapest.

Summary

Equivalent ratios

In this chapter you have looked at various ways of writing ratios.

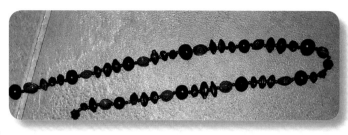

In this necklace you can see a repeating pattern of black, red, brown, brown, brown; black, red, brown, brown, brown.

The ratio of black : red : brown is 1 : 1 : 3.

It is also possible to see a black : red : brown ratio of 2 : 2 : 6.

There are several other ways of seeing the ratio, such as 8 : 8 : 24.

The ratios: 8 : 8 : 24
    and   2 : 2 : 6
    and   1 : 1 : 3
    are all equivalent ratios.

1 : 1 : 3 is the **simplified ratio** of 8 : 8 : 24.

Sharing in a given ratio

You learned how to use the **rectangular bar model** to share out quantities in a particular ratio.

In the problem below, Kate and Pam were sharing the cost of their £9.50 pizza in the ratio 2 : 3.

Kate first drew a rectangular block.

She split it into five parts (two parts and three parts).

She then figured out the cost for each part and worked out a cost for two parts and for three parts.

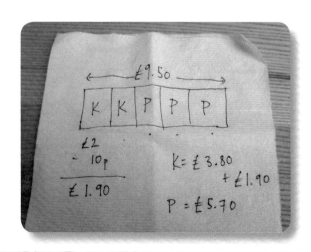

Using a ratio table

You saw several situations where a ratio table could help you solve a problem.

The ratio table below was used to work out how many of each type of bead would be needed in a necklace of 150 beads in total.

Rectangle	1	10	20	5	25
Links	4	40	80	20	100
Oval	1	10	20	5	25
Total	6	60	120	30	150

The ratio table below was used to see how far a greyhound doing 400 metres in $22\frac{1}{2}$ seconds would go in 1 second.

Metres	400	800	160	17 and a bit
Seconds	$22\frac{1}{2}$	45	9	1

A ratio table is a really helpful tool to solve many problems in many topic areas, not just those that obviously mention ratios.

Martha making sense of multiplication

1. Martha's little sister is in primary school and she is currently learning about multiplication of whole numbers. In her exercise book she has written:

6 × 5 = 6 + 6 + 6 + 6 + 6   6 × 5 = 5 + 5 + 5 + 5 + 5 + 5

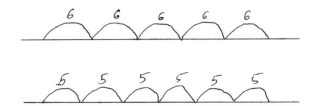

She also wrote: '6 × 5 is 6 lots of 5 or 5 lots of 6'.

Do 5 lots of 6 give the same answer as 6 lots of 5?

2. Martha was in her own school the next day and by coincidence she was asked to do some multiplications. She remembered looking at her sister's exercise book and decided to use her sister's approach. She also told her friends about it.

a) Use Martha's sister's number line sketch and 'lots of' statement to illustrate each of the following:

i)   2 × 5

ii)   15 × 4

iii)   3 × 2.5

iv)   3.25 × 4

v) $6 \times \frac{1}{2}$

vi) $3\frac{1}{4} \times 4$

vii) $\frac{3}{4} \times 8$

viii)   2.5 × 2.5

b)

Which way do you see it?

c) Martha wrote the following in her exercise book:

viii) 2¹/₂ lots of 2¹/₂

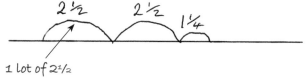

1 lot of 2¹/₂

So the answer is 6¹/₄

Explain Martha's approach and how she got $6\frac{1}{4}$.

d) Try the following questions by drawing a number line and using the 'lots of' idea above:

i)   2.5 lots of 6

ii)   1.5 lots of $2\frac{1}{2}$

iii) 2.5 × 4.4

iv) $2\frac{1}{4}$ × 4.8

v)   6.2 × 4.5

vi) $2\frac{1}{4}$ × 2.4

3 **a)** Some people prefer to use a ratio table to do multiplication. So, for example, 23×46 can be done like this:

1	10	20	3	23
46	460	920	138	1058

Explain how this has been done.

b) Other people prefer grid multiplication:

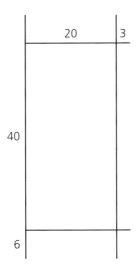

Copy and fill in this grid and write down the answer to 23×46.

4 As decimal multiplications get more complicated (e.g. 2.58 × 3.27) it is recommended that you do the calculation as if they were whole numbers (e.g. 258 × 327) and then use estimation to decide where to put the decimal point.

Here is how Mamta did the above calculation:

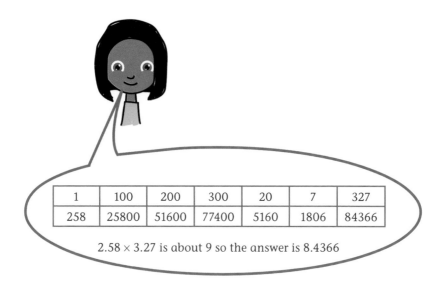

1	100	200	300	20	7	327
258	25800	51600	77400	5160	1806	84366

2.58 × 3.27 is about 9 so the answer is 8.4366

a) Can you see how she worked out that the answer was about 9?
b) Work out:
   i)   2.35 × 4.1
   ii) 5.26 × 12.1
   iii) 6.23 × 4.52

Does multiplication make the answer bigger?

2 x 4 = 8

Yes, it does work

1 x 5 = 5

No, it doesn't

5 a) Use a calculator to work out the following:

   i) 5×10

   ii) 5×8

   iii) 0.5×10

   iv) 0.1×18

   v) 1×6

   vi) $\frac{3}{4} \times 4$

   vii) $2\frac{1}{2} \times 8$

   viii) 5×4

   ix) 0.25×8

b) Can you see when multiplication makes the answer bigger, when the answer stays the same, and when it makes the answer smaller?

c) Can you explain why sometimes multiplication makes the answer smaller?

Multiplying fractions

6 A question in a maths test is: 'What is $\frac{2}{3} \times \frac{3}{4}$?'

Some people are happy to work out $\frac{2}{3}$ of $\frac{3}{4}$ or $\frac{3}{4}$ of $\frac{2}{3}$ by, say, drawing a number line $\frac{2}{3}$ long and dividing it into quarters and then working out $\frac{3}{4}$ of $\frac{2}{3}$. Here is David's attempt:

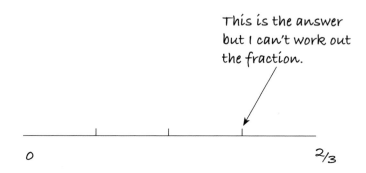

This is the answer but I can't work out the fraction.

0   2/3

Although the idea is reasonable, it is often difficult to see the answer.

If it becomes too difficult to work these out using the number line idea, then another approach is possible.

If you look back at Chapter 1 of this book you will see that when Coley was working out how to add and subtract fractions he imagined that he had a pizza cut into a convenient number of slices.

He tried this approach with $\frac{2}{3} \times \frac{3}{4}$.

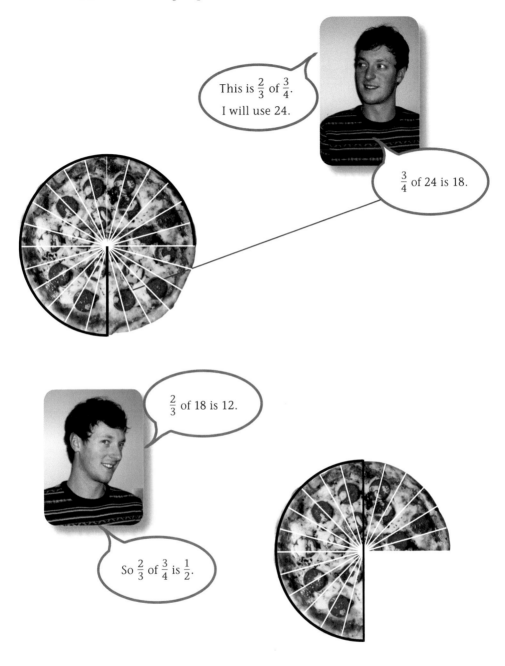

This is $\frac{2}{3}$ of $\frac{3}{4}$.
I will use 24.

$\frac{3}{4}$ of 24 is 18.

$\frac{2}{3}$ of 18 is 12.

So $\frac{2}{3}$ of $\frac{3}{4}$ is $\frac{1}{2}$.

Look at Coley's work on 'What is $\frac{2}{3}$ of $\frac{3}{4}$ of 24?'

Where did Coley get the answer $\frac{1}{2}$?

 Complete Workbook exercise 4.1 on page 33 of your workbook.

Understanding division

7 How would you do the following problems?

   a) A school is organising a trip for 258 students. It needs to hire minibuses each holding 24 students and a teacher. How many minibuses will be needed?

   b) Because a class did really well, their teacher brought in 258 sweets to share between the 24 students. How many sweets does each student get?

   In each case draw a diagram to represent the problems.

   Can you represent your solution on a number line?

8 Here is another problem:

   12 metres of ribbon is to be shared between two people.

   How long will each piece be?

   This could be represented like this:

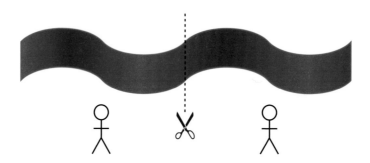

   How many 2 metre strips could you cut from 12 metres of ribbon?

   This could be represented like this:

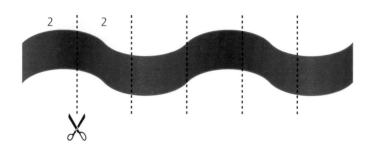

So essentially a division problem can usually be seen in two ways:

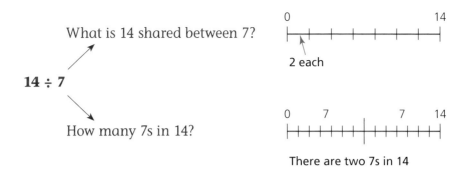

What is 14 shared between 7?

14 ÷ 7

How many 7s in 14?

a) In each case show how the question relates to the number line.
b) Could you explain how to do $6 \div \frac{1}{2}$ using the same method as part **a)**?

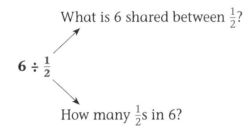

What is 6 shared between $\frac{1}{2}$?

$6 \div \frac{1}{2}$

How many $\frac{1}{2}$s in 6?

  Complete Workbook exercise 4.2 on page 34 of your workbook.

Does division make the answer smaller?

When you are sharing it must make the answer smaller.

Sharing is just one way of seeing division. You can't share 4 apples between $\frac{1}{2}$ a person.

9 a) Use a calculator to work out the following:

    i) $8 \div 2$

    ii) $16 \div \frac{1}{2}$

    iii) $16 \div 3$

    iv) $10 \div 0.1$

    v) $12 \div 1$

    vi) $12 \div 1\frac{1}{2}$

    vii) $5 \div 0.2$

b) Can you see when the answer is bigger, when it stays the same, and when it is smaller?

c) Can you explain why sometimes division makes the answer bigger?

Mixing it up

10 Although most people think of fractions, decimals and percentages as very different, they are really the same idea written in different ways.

So, for example, the fraction $\frac{1}{4}$ is the same as 25%, which is the same as the decimal 0.25. For numbers bigger than one we can also use all three. For example, $1\frac{1}{2}$ is 150%, which is the same as 1.5.

We tend to choose the one that best suits the problem we are solving or the context we are working in.

So, for example:

a) Which would you be more likely to say?

Was £~~150~~
Now £75

That's a 0.25 discount.

That's a $\frac{1}{4}$ discount.

That's a 25% discount.

b) Which would you be more likely to say?

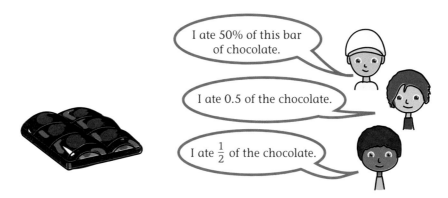

I ate 50% of this bar of chocolate.

I ate 0.5 of the chocolate.

I ate $\frac{1}{2}$ of the chocolate.

c) Your teacher asks how certain you are that the answer you've just given is correct. Which response is more likely if you feel confident about your answer?

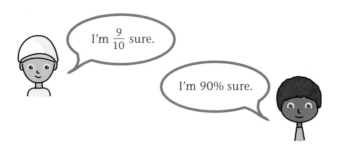

d) On a talent show the judge is deciding whether to vote a contestant off. Which do you think you are more likely to hear the contestant say?

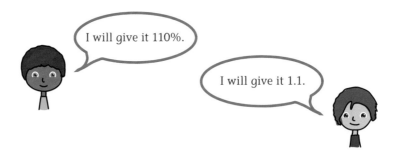

But if you were asked to work out 50% of 40, you might say that this is the same as $\frac{1}{2}$ of 40 to help you work it out.

To work out 4 × 2.5, some people would think this is 4 lots of $2\frac{1}{2}$.

So the ability to swap between decimals, fractions and percentages can be very helpful.

11 **a)** Copy out the following table and see what you can fill in without much effort.

Decimal	Fraction	Percentage
1		
0.75		
	$\frac{1}{2}$	
		$33\frac{1}{3}\%$
0.25		
0.2		
		10%

b) Which of these was most difficult?

c) Work out the following. (Sometimes it will help to use the table above to convert.)

   i) $0.75 + \frac{1}{4}$ **ii)** $\frac{1}{2} \times 10\%$

  iii) $33\frac{1}{3}\% + \frac{2}{3}$ **iv)** $1.5 \times 200\%$

   v) $0.1 + \frac{1}{4}$ **vi)** 250% of 40

  vii) $\frac{3}{4} - 25\%$ **viii)** $2\frac{1}{2} \times 0.5$

   ix) $0.75 - \frac{1}{2}$ **x)** $\frac{1}{2}$ of $33\frac{1}{3}\%$

   xi) $0.5 \times \frac{1}{2}$

d) Put the following in order on a number line using the table above.

   i) $\frac{1}{4}$, 0.5, 10%, $\frac{4}{5}$, $\frac{7}{8}$

  ii) 25%, 0.6, 1.2, $\frac{3}{4}$, 30%

  iii) $\frac{2}{3}$, $\frac{1}{2}$, 0.9, 75%, 1, 0

Summary

In this chapter you have looked at different ways you can understand multiplication and division when the numbers are not whole.

You also saw how an understanding of the relationship between fractions, decimals and percentages can help you to solve more difficult problems.